What is black and white and red all over?

Clifford dressed up as a zebra.

NORMAN BRIDWELL
Clifford's RIDDLES

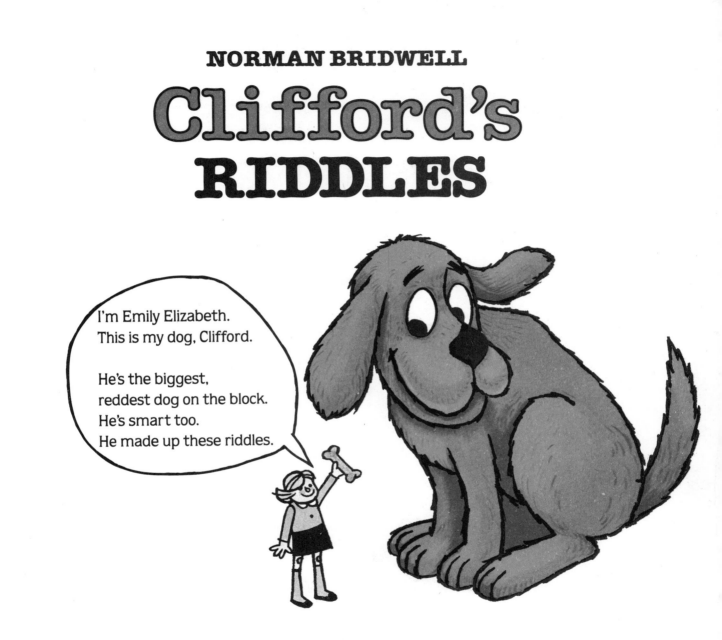

I'm Emily Elizabeth.
This is my dog, Clifford.

He's the biggest,
reddest dog on the block.
He's smart too.
He made up these riddles.

SCHOLASTIC INC.
New York   Toronto   London   Auckland   Sydney

To Christopher and Paul

ISBN 0-590-97435-1

12 11 10 9 8 7 6 5 4 3 2 1   1   6 7 8 9/9 0 1/0

Printed in the U.S.A.   24

What is wet and pink

and holds fifty cans of dog food?

Clifford's tongue.

What is twelve feet tall,
stops at stop lights,
and has training wheels?

Clifford's bicycle.

Name two kinds of wood you would use
if you made a statue of Clifford.

Giant redwood and dogwood.

If a dog marries a very small fish,
what will their baby be?

A guppy puppy.

If a bloodhound marries a bat,
what will their child be?

A vampire dog.

What did Clifford do to get rid of dog pounds?

He went on a diet.

It's sweet. It's furry. It barks.
And it's frozen on a stick.
What is it?

A pup-sicle.

What do you call a wet pup?

A soggy doggy.

If your dog kisses you,
what do you call it?

A pooch smooch.

What would be a good job for Clifford?

He could be a Seeing Eye dog for King Kong.

Where do you find bullies
who pick on Clifford's friends?

Far, far away.

It's safe when it's sad.

But when it's happy — watch out!

What is it?

Clifford's tail.

What floats on water, is yellow,
goes "quack, quack,"
and weighs a hundred pounds?

Clifford's rubber ducky.

He is faster than a speeding greyhound.
He is stronger than a Great Dane.
And he can leap over a dog catcher
in a single bound.
Who is he?

Super Pooch.